ROYAL GEOGRAPHICAL SOCIETY
*WITH THE INSTITUTE OF BRITISH GEOGRAPHERS*

# travel journal

FRANCES LINCOLN

Frances Lincoln Limited
4 Torriano Mews
Torriano Avenue
London NW5 2RZ

Royal Geographical Society Travel Journal
Published in association with the Royal Geographical Society
Copyright © Frances Lincoln Limited 2001
Introduction copyright © Royal Geographical Society
All photographs copyright © Chris Caldicott

British Library cataloguing-in-publication data
A catalogue record for this book is available
from the British Library

Cover design conceived by Annabel Fraser
Designed by Becky Clarke

ISBN 0 7112 1775 0

Printed in Hong Kong
First Frances Lincoln edition 2001

The Royal Geographical Society Picture Library is a commercial
enterprise, specializing in exploration and geographical images
from 1830 to the present day. The library contains over 500,000
photographs and paintings providing geographical, historical
and social information in pictorial form. This notable
collection contains images from early Everest expeditions,
Thomas Baines' paintings of Livingstone's travels, beautiful
illustrated maps from every corner of the globe, artefacts
which include Darwin's sextant and Shackleton's balaclava as
well as modern colour slides depicting a variety of areas and
people of the world.

TITLE PAGE: *La Digue Island, Seychelles*

# INTRODUCTION

The Royal Geographical Society (with the Institute of British Geographers) was founded in 1830 and given a Royal Charter in 1859 for 'the advancement of geographical science'. The Society is a leading world centre for geographical learning, supporting and promoting many aspects of geography. These include geographical research, education and teaching, field training and small expeditions, the public understanding and popularization of geography and the provision of geographical information. The Society holds historical collections of national and international importance, many of which relate to the Society's association with, and support for, scientific exploration and research from the nineteenth century onwards.

It was pivotal in establishing geography as a teaching and research discipline in British universities towards the end of the nineteenth and in the early years of the twentieth centuries and has played a key role in geographical and environmental education ever since.

Membership of the Society encompasses professional geographers, students and geography enthusiasts with a keen interest in the diverse peoples, places, cultures and environments of our world. The Society welcomes those interested in geography as members. Please visit the website at http://www.rgs.org for further information.

Dr Andrew Tatham
Head of Information Resources

# USING THIS BOOK

Every journey needs some organization and with a little planning before you set out, valuable time can be saved when you are *en route*. This journal is the ideal place to list your travel arrangements – train times, flight numbers and other essential information – together with recommendations for places to visit, stay or eat, gathered from friends or guidebooks. Using this book, your time can be as carefully planned or as spontaneous as you wish.

The 'Journal' section is the place to write about your experiences or to make sketches of the places you explore: the sights and sounds, the unfolding landscapes, the people you meet and the discoveries you make.

At the back of the book, you will find conversion tables and useful information about countries you may visit or pass through, as well as space to keep track of budgets and make a note of useful addresses.

# PERSONAL DETAILS

name

address

telephone no.

fax no.

mobile no.

e-mail address

passport no.

driving licence no.

in case of emergency, please contact

name

address

telephone no.

Amalfi Coast, Italy

dates

place

_____ to _____

_____ to _____

_____ to _____

_____ to _____

_____ to _____

_____ to _____

_____ to _____

_____ to _____

_____ to _____

_____ to _____

# ITINERARIES

dates                    place

_____ to _____    _____

_____ to _____    _____

_____ to _____    _____

_____ to _____    _____

_____ to _____    _____

_____ to _____    _____

_____ to _____    _____

_____ to _____    _____

_____ to _____    _____

_____ to _____    _____

_____ to _____    _____

_____ to _____    _____

_____ to _____    _____

*Corniglia, Italy*

# ITINERARIES

dates

place

____ to ____

____ to ____

____ to ____

____ to ____

____ to ____

____ to ____

____ to ____

____ to ____

____ to ____

____ to ____

____ to ____

____ to ____

# ITINERARIES

dates            place

_____ to _____      _____

_____ to _____      _____

_____ to _____      _____

_____ to _____      _____

_____ to _____      _____

_____ to _____      _____

_____ to _____      _____

_____ to _____      _____

_____ to _____      _____

_____ to _____      _____

_____ to _____      _____

_____ to _____      _____

_____ to _____      _____

*New York, U.S.A.*

# ITINERARIES

dates                          place

___ to ___

___ to ___

___ to ___

___ to ___

___ to ___

___ to ___

___ to ___

___ to ___

___ to ___

___ to ___

___ to ___

___ to ___

*The Niger, Mali*

dates                                    place

_____ to _____    ............................................................................

_____ to _____    ............................................................................

_____ to _____    ............................................................................

_____ to _____    ............................................................................

_____ to _____    ............................................................................

_____ to _____    ............................................................................

_____ to _____    ............................................................................

_____ to _____    ............................................................................

_____ to _____    ............................................................................

_____ to _____    ............................................................................

date

details

# PLACES TO VISIT

date

details

The Sahara Desert, Mali

# PLACES TO VISIT

date

details

# PLACES TO VISIT

date                    details

*Hong Kong*

# PLACES TO VISIT

date

details

*La Digue Island, Seychelles*

# PLACES TO VISIT

date

details

# PLACES TO STAY

### name

### address/telephone

*Paxos, Greece*

# PLACES TO STAY

| name | address/telephone | notes |
|------|-------------------|-------|
|      |                   |       |

# PLACES TO STAY

| name | address/telephone | notes |
|------|-------------------|-------|
|      |                   |       |

# PLACES TO STAY

| name | address/telephone | notes |
|------|-------------------|-------|
|      |                   |       |

*Jaisalmer, India*

# PLACES TO STAY

| name | address/telephone | notes |
|------|-------------------|-------|
|      |                   |       |
|      |                   |       |
|      |                   |       |
|      |                   |       |
|      |                   |       |
|      |                   |       |
|      |                   |       |
|      |                   |       |
|      |                   |       |

# PLACES TO STAY

name                     address/telephone

*Riomaggiore, Italy*

# PLACES TO EAT

name          address/telephone          notes

*Lombok, Indonesia*

# PLACES TO EAT

| name | address/telephone | notes |
| --- | --- | --- |
| | | |
| | | |
| | | |
| | | |
| | | |
| | | |
| | | |

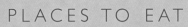

# PLACES TO EAT

name address/telephone

*Marrakesh, Morocco*

# PLACES TO EAT

name        address/telephone        notes

| name | address/telephone | notes |
|------|-------------------|-------|
| | | |
| | | |
| | | |
| | | |
| | | |
| | | |
| | | |

# PLACES TO EAT

| name | address/telephone | notes |
| --- | --- | --- |
| | | |

*Vilcabamba, Ecuador*

# JOURNAL

*Atacama Desert, Chile*

Sonepur, India

*Maymyo, Burma*

Paxos, Greece

Lomas de Lachay National Reserve, Peru

JOURNAL

Moscow, Russia

*Rio de Janeiro, Brazil*

Mount Everest, Nepal

Aspen, Colorado, U.S.A.

*Campania, Italy*

Serengeti Plain, Tanzania

*Rio de Janeiro, Brazil*

Atlas Mountains, Morocco

Jaipur, India

*Costa Rica*

# BUDGETS

| date | details | amount | |
|------|---------|--------|--|
|      |         |        |  |
|      |         |        |  |
|      |         |        |  |
|      |         |        |  |
|      |         |        |  |
|      |         |        |  |
|      |         |        |  |
|      |         |        |  |
|      |         |        |  |
|      |         |        |  |
|      |         |        |  |
|      |         |        |  |

# BUDGETS

| date | details | amount | |
|------|---------|--------|--|
|      |         |        |  |
|      |         |        |  |
|      |         |        |  |
|      |         |        |  |
|      |         |        |  |
|      |         |        |  |
|      |         |        |  |
|      |         |        |  |
|      |         |        |  |

# BUDGETS

| date | details | amount | |
|------|---------|--------|---|
|      |         |        |   |
|      |         |        |   |
|      |         |        |   |
|      |         |        |   |
|      |         |        |   |
|      |         |        |   |
|      |         |        |   |
|      |         |        |   |
|      |         |        |   |
|      |         |        |   |
|      |         |        |   |
|      |         |        |   |

# BUDGETS

| date | details | amount | |
|------|---------|--------|--|
| | | | |
| | | | |
| | | | |
| | | | |
| | | | |
| | | | |
| | | | |
| | | | |
| | | | |
| | | | |

# BUDGETS

| date | details | amount | |
|------|---------|--------|---|
|      |         |        |   |
|      |         |        |   |
|      |         |        |   |
|      |         |        |   |
|      |         |        |   |
|      |         |        |   |
|      |         |        |   |
|      |         |        |   |
|      |         |        |   |
|      |         |        |   |
|      |         |        |   |
|      |         |        |   |

# BUDGETS

| date | details | amount | |
|------|---------|--------|--|
| | | | |
| | | | |
| | | | |
| | | | |
| | | | |
| | | | |
| | | | |
| | | | |
| | | | |
| | | | |

| country | dialling code | hours diff. from GMT | country | dialling code | hours diff. from GMT |
|---|---|---|---|---|---|
| Afghanistan | 93 | +4½ | Chad | 235 | +1 |
| Albania | 355 | +1 | Chile | 56 | −4 |
| Algeria | 213 | +1 | China | 86 | +8 |
| Andorra | 376 | +1 | Christmas Island | 61 | +7 |
| Angola | 244 | +1 | Colombia | 57 | −5 |
| Anguilla | 1264 | −4 | Comoros | 269 | +3 |
| Antigua and Barbuda | 1268 | −4 | Congo | 242 | +1 |
| Argentina | 54 | −3 | Cook Islands | 682 | −10½ |
| Armenia | 374 | +4 | Costa Rica | 506 | −6 |
| Aruba | 297 | −4 | Côte d' Ivoire | 225 | 0 |
| Ascension Island | 247 | 0 | Croatia | 385 | +1 |
| Australia | 61 | +8/+10 | Cuba | 53 | −5 |
| Austria | 43 | +1 | Cyprus | 357/90392 | +2 |
| Azerbaijan | 994 | +5 | Czech Republic | 420 | +1 |
| Bahamas | 1242 | −5 | Denmark | 45 | +1 |
| Bahrain | 973 | +3 | Diego Garcia | 246 | +5 |
| Bangladesh | 880 | +6 | Djibouti | 253 | +3 |
| Barbados | 1246 | −4 | Dominica | 1767 | −4 |
| Belarus | 375 | +2 | Dominican Republic | 1809 | −4 |
| Belgium | 32 | +1 | Ecuador | 593 | −5 |
| Belize | 501 | −6 | Egypt | 20 | +2 |
| Benin | 229 | +1 | El Salvador | 503 | −6 |
| Bermuda | 1441 | −4 | Equatorial Guinea | 240 | +1 |
| Bhutan | 975 | +6 | Eritrea | 291 | +3 |
| Bolivia | 591 | −4 | Estonia | 372 | +2 |
| Bosnia-Herzegovina | 387 | +1 | Ethiopia | 251 | +3 |
| Botswana | 267 | +2 | Falkland Islands | 500 | −4 |
| Brazil | 55 | −3 | Faroe Islands | 298 | 0 |
| Brunei | 673 | +8 | Fiji | 679 | +12 |
| Bulgaria | 359 | +2 | Finland | 358 | +2 |
| Burkina Faso | 226 | 0 | France | 33 | +1 |
| Burundi | 257 | +2 | French Guiana | 594 | −3 |
| Cambodia | 855 | +7 | French Polynesia | 689 | −10 |
| Cameroon | 237 | +1 | Gabon | 241 | +1 |
| Canada | 1 | −3½/−8 | Gambia | 220 | 0 |
| Cape Verde | 238 | −1 | Georgia | 995 | +4 |
| Cayman Islands | 1345 | −5 | Germany | 49 | +1 |
| Central African Republic | 236 | +1 | Ghana | 233 | 0 |
| | | | Gibraltar | 350 | +1 |

# INTERNATIONAL INFORMATION

| country | dialling code | hours diff. from GMT | country | dialling code | hours diff. from GMT |
|---|---|---|---|---|---|
| Greece | 30 | +2 | Macedonia | 389 | +1 |
| Greenland | 299 | −4 | Madagascar | 261 | +3 |
| Grenada | 1473 | −4 | Malawi | 265 | +2 |
| Guadeloupe | 590 | −4 | Malaysia | 60 | +8 |
| Guam | 671 | +10 | Maldives | 960 | +5 |
| Guatemala | 502 | −6 | Mali | 223 | 0 |
| Guinea | 224 | 0 | Malta | 356 | +1 |
| Guinea-Bissau | 245 | 0 | Marshall Islands | 692 | +12 |
| Guyana | 592 | −4 | Martinique | 596 | −4 |
| Haiti | 509 | −5 | Mauritania | 222 | 0 |
| Honduras | 504 | −6 | Mauritius | 230 | +4 |
| Hong Kong | 852 | +8 | Mayotte | 269 | +3 |
| Hungary | 36 | +1 | Mexico | 52 | −6/−7 |
| Iceland | 354 | 0 | Micronesia | 691 | +10/+11 |
| India | 91 | +5½ | Moldova | 373 | +1½ |
| Indonesia | 62 | +7/+8 | Monaco | 377 | +1 |
| Iran | 98 | +3½ | Mongolia | 976 | +8 |
| Iraq | 964 | +3 | Montserrat | 1664 | −4 |
| Ireland | 353 | 0 | Morocco | 212 | 0 |
| Israel | 972 | +2 | Mozambique | 258 | +2 |
| Italy | 39 | +1 | Myanmar | 95 | +6½ |
| Jamaica | 1876 | −5 | Namibia | 264 | +2 |
| Japan | 81 | +9 | Nauru | 674 | +12 |
| Jordon | 962 | +2 | Nepal | 977 | +5¾ |
| Kazakhstan | 7 | +5/+6 | Netherlands | 31 | +1 |
| Kenya | 254 | +3 | Netherlands Antilles | 599 | −4 |
| Kiribati | 686 | +12 | New Caledonia | 687 | +11 |
| Kuwait | 965 | +3 | New Zealand | 64 | +12 |
| Kyrgyzstan | 996 | +6 | Nicaragua | 505 | −6 |
| Laos | 856 | +7 | Niger | 227 | +1 |
| Latvia | 371 | +2 | Nigeria | 234 | +1 |
| Lebanon | 961 | +2 | Niue | 683 | −11 |
| Lesotho | 266 | +2 | Norfolk Island | 672 | +11½ |
| Liberia | 231 | 0 | Northern Marianas | 670 | +10 |
| Libya | 218 | +1 | North Korea | 850 | +9 |
| Liechtenstein | 4175 | +1 | Norway | 47 | +1 |
| Lithuania | 370 | +2 | Oman | 968 | +4 |
| Luxembourg | 352 | +1 | Pakistan | 92 | +5 |
| Macao | 853 | +8 | Palau | 680 | +9 |

| country | dialling code | hours diff. from GMT | country | dialling code | hours diff. from GMT |
|---|---|---|---|---|---|
| Panama | 507 | −5 | Surinam | 597 | −3 |
| Papua New Guinea | 675 | +10 | Swaziland | 268 | +2 |
| Paraguay | 595 | −4 | Sweden | 46 | +1 |
| Peru | 51 | −5 | Switzerland | 41 | +1 |
| Philippines | 63 | +8 | Syria | 963 | +2 |
| Poland | 48 | +1 | Taiwan | 886 | +8 |
| Portugal | 351 | 0 | Tajikistan | 7 | +5 |
| Puerto Rico | 1787 | −4 | Tanzania | 255 | +3 |
| Qatar | 974 | +3 | Thailand | 66 | +7 |
| Réunion | 262 | +4 | Togo | 228 | 0 |
| Romania | 40 | +2 | Tonga | 676 | +13 |
| Russian Federation | 7 | +2/+12 | Trinidad and Tobago | 1868 | −4 |
| Rwanda | 250 | +2 | Tristan da Cunha | 2897 | −1 |
| St Helena | 290 | 0 | Tunisia | 216 | +1 |
| St Kitts and Nevis | 1869 | −4 | Turkey | 90 | +2 |
| St Lucia | 1758 | −4 | Turkmenistan | 993 | +5 |
| St Pierre and Miquelon | 508 | −3 | Turks and Caicos Islands | 1649 | −5 |
| St Vincent and the Grenadines | 1784 | −4 | Tuvalu | 688 | +12 |
| Samoa (USA) | 684 | −11 | Uganda | 256 | +3 |
| Samoa (Western) | 685 | −11 | Ukraine | 380 | +2 |
| San Marino | 378 | +1 | United Arab Emirates | 971 | +4 |
| São Tomé and Principe | 239 | 0 | United Kingdom | 44 | 0 |
| Saudi Arabia | 966 | +3 | United States of America | 1 | −5/−11 |
| Senegal | 221 | 0 | Uruguay | 598 | −3 |
| Seychelles | 248 | +4 | Uzbekistan | 7 | +5/+6 |
| Sierra Leone | 232 | 0 | Vanuatu | 678 | +11 |
| Singapore | 65 | +8 | Venezuela | 58 | −4 |
| Slovakia | 421 | +1 | Vietnam | 84 | +7 |
| Slovenia | 386 | +1 | Virgin Islands (UK) | 1284 | −4 |
| Solomon Islands | 677 | +11 | Virgin Islands (US) | 1340 | −4 |
| Somalia | 252 | +3 | Western Samoa | 685 | −11 |
| South Africa | 27 | +2 | Yemen | 967 | +3 |
| South Korea | 82 | +9 | Yugoslavia | 381 | +1 |
| Spain | 34 | +1 | Zaïre | 243 | +1 |
| Sri Lanka | 94 | +5½ | Zambia | 260 | +2 |
| Sudan | 249 | +2 | Zimbabwe | 263 | +2 |

# CONVERSION TABLES

## centimetres to inches

| cm | | inches |
|---|---|---|
| 2.54 | 1 | 0.39 |
| 5.08 | 2 | 0.79 |
| 7.62 | 3 | 1.81 |
| 10.1 | 4 | 1.57 |
| 12.7 | 5 | 1.97 |
| 15.2 | 6 | 2.36 |
| 17.8 | 7 | 2.76 |
| 20.3 | 8 | 3.15 |
| 22.9 | 9 | 3.54 |
| 25.4 | 10 | 3.94 |
| 27.9 | 11 | 4.33 |
| 30.4 | 12 | 4.72 |

## litres to gallons

| litres | | gallons |
|---|---|---|
| 4.5 | 1 | 0.22 |
| 9.1 | 2 | 0.44 |
| 13.6 | 3 | 0.66 |
| 18.2 | 4 | 0.88 |
| 22.7 | 5 | 1.10 |
| 27.3 | 6 | 1.32 |
| 31.8 | 7 | 1.54 |
| 36.4 | 8 | 1.76 |
| 40.9 | 9 | 1.98 |
| 45.5 | 10 | 2.20 |

## men's suits and overcoats

| American | British | Continental |
|---|---|---|
| 36 | 36 | 46 |
| 38 | 38 | 48 |
| 40 | 40 | 50 |
| 42 | 42 | 52 |
| 44 | 44 | 54 |

## women's shoes

| American | British | Continental |
|---|---|---|
| 6 | 4 | 38 |
| 7 | 5 | 39 |
| 8 | 6 | 40 |
| 9 | 7 | 41 |
| 10 | 8 | 42 |

## metres to feet

| metres | | feet |
|---|---|---|
| 0.30 | 1 | 3.3 |
| 0.61 | 2 | 6.6 |
| 0.91 | 3 | 9.8 |
| 1.22 | 4 | 13.1 |
| 1.52 | 5 | 16.4 |
| 1.83 | 6 | 19.7 |
| 2.13 | 7 | 23.0 |
| 2.44 | 8 | 26.2 |
| 2.74 | 9 | 29.5 |
| 3.05 | 10 | 32.8 |

## celsius to fahrenheit

| °c | °f |
|---|---|
| -10 | 14 |
| -5 | 23 |
| 0 | 32 |
| 5 | 41 |
| 10 | 50 |
| 15 | 59 |
| 20 | 68 |
| 25 | 77 |
| 30 | 86 |
| 35 | 95 |
| 40 | 104 |
| 45 | 113 |
| 50 | 122 |

## women's suits and dresses

| American | British | Continental |
|---|---|---|
| 6 | 8 | 36 |
| 8 | 10 | 38 |
| 10 | 12 | 40 |
| 12 | 14 | 42 |
| 14 | 16 | 44 |
| 16 | 18 | 46 |
| 18 | 20 | 48 |

## kilograms to pounds

| kg | | lb |
|---|---|---|
| 0.45 | 1 | 2.2 |
| 0.91 | 2 | 4.4 |
| 1.36 | 3 | 6.6 |
| 1.81 | 4 | 8.8 |
| 2.27 | 5 | 11.0 |
| 2.72 | 6 | 13.2 |
| 3.18 | 7 | 15.4 |
| 3.63 | 8 | 17.6 |
| 4.08 | 9 | 19.8 |
| 4.54 | 10 | 22.0 |

## kilometres to miles

| km | miles |
|---|---|
| 10 | 6.2 |
| 20 | 12.4 |
| 30 | 18.6 |
| 40 | 24.9 |
| 50 | 31.1 |
| 60 | 37.3 |
| 70 | 43.5 |
| 80 | 49.5 |
| 90 | 55.9 |
| 100 | 62.1 |

## men's shoes

| American | British | Continental |
|---|---|---|
| 8 | 7 | 40 |
| 9 | 8 | 41 |
| 10 | 9 | 42 |
| 11 | 10 | 43 |
| 12 | 11 | 44 |
| 13 | 12 | 45 |

## men's shirts

| American | British | Continental |
|---|---|---|
| 14 | 14 | 36 |
| 14½ | 14½ | 37 |
| 15 | 15 | 38 |
| 15½ | 15½ | 39 |
| 16 | 16 | 41 |
| 16½ | 16½ | 42 |
| 17 | 17 | 43 |

*Serengeti Plain, Tanzania*

Kakum National Park, Ghana

# USEFUL ADDRESSES

*Luxor, Egypt*